JAMES ALLEN
THE LIFE TRIUMPHANT

Mastering the Heart and Mind

CLASSICS

First published in 1908

Published 2022
FiNGERPRINT! CLASSICS
An imprint of Prakash Books India Pvt. Ltd.

113/A, Darya Ganj,
New Delhi-110 002
Tel: (011) 2324 7062 – 65, Fax: (011) 2324 6975
Email: info@prakashbooks.com/sales@prakashbooks.com

www.facebook.com/fingerprintpublishing
www.twitter.com/FingerprintP
www.fingerprintpublishing.com

ISBN: 978 93 5440 102 2

Processed & printed in India by HT Media Ltd, Greater Noida

James Allen was born to William and Martha Allen on 28 November 1864 in Leicester, England. After a decline in trade in 1879, William, a stocking framework knitter, went to America to start afresh. But before he could settle his family there, he was robbed and murdered.

Being the elder son of the family, Allen had to take the family's responsibility. He was forced to leave school and find a job. In the following years, he worked for many British manufacturing firms as a stationer and private secretary. At the age of twenty-nine, he travelled to London and then to South Wales, where he worked as a journalist and reporter.

Allen married Lily Louisa Oram in 1895. Three years later, he began working as a writer for the magazine *The Herald of the Golden Age*. His first book, *From Poverty to Power*, was written and published in 1901, when he was thirty-seven. He described this book as "A book for all those who are in search of better conditions, wider freedom, and increased usefulness." The following year, Allen started a spiritual magazine titled *The Light of Reason*. It was later renamed *The Epoch*. *All These Things Added* (1903) was his second book.

As a Man Thinketh, Allen's third book, was published in 1903. Serving as a source of inspiration for many, *As a Man Thinketh* is one of his most famous and bestselling works. It describes the way our thoughts impact our lives. We tend to become what we think.

Allen moved to Ilfracombe in 1903 along with his family and spent the rest of his life there. He published numerous works among which are: *Out from the Heart* (1904), *Morning and Evening Thoughts* (1909), *The Mastery of Destiny* (1909), *Above Life's Turmoil* (1910), *From Passion to Peace* (1910), *Eight Pillars of Prosperity* (1911), *Light on Life's Difficulties* (1912), *The Shining Gateway* (1915), and *The Divine Companion* (1919).

In 1908, Allen published *The Life Triumphant: Mastering the Heart and Mind*, an essential guide that shows how to emerge victorious over "the dark things of life" and re-establish a firm hold over one's heart and mind, thereby achieving true success and happiness.

Allen died on 24 January 1912, aged forty-seven. He is considered as one of the founding fathers of modern inspirational thought.

Contents

Foreword   *9*

1. Faith and Courage   11
2. Manliness, Womanliness and Sincerity   21
3. Energy and Power   31
4. Self-Control and Happiness   41
5. Simplicity and Freedom   51
6. Right Thinking and Repose   59
7. Calmness and Resource   69
8. Insight and Nobility   79
9. Man the Master   89
10. Knowledge and Victory   97

Foreword

Every being lives in his own mental world. His joys and sorrows are the creations of his own mind, and are dependent upon the mind for their existence. In the midst of the world, darkened with many sins and sorrows, in which the majority live, there abides another world, lighted up with shining virtues and unpolluted joy, in which the perfect ones live. This world can be found and entered, and the way to it is by self-control and moral excellence. It is the world of the perfect life, and it rightly belongs to man, who is not complete until crowned with perfection. The perfect life is not the faraway, impossible thing that men who are in darkness imagine it to be; it is supremely possible, and very near and real. Man remains a craving, weeping, sinning, repenting creature just so long as he wills to do so by clinging to those weak conditions. But when he wills to shake off his dark dreams and to rise, he arises and achieves.

James Allen

Hail to Thee, Man divine! the conqueror
Of sin and shame and sorrow; no more weak,
Wormlike, and groveling art thou; no, nor
Wilt thou again bow down to things that weak
Scourgings and death upon thee; thou dost rise
Triumphant in thy strength; good, pure and wise.

1
Faith and Courage

For those who will fight bravely and not yield, there is triumphant victory over all the dark things of life. I state this at the beginning, that the reader may know there is no uncertainty about it. In the course of this book I shall show what are the elements, in character and conduct, which go to build up the life of calm strength and superlative victory.

To stand face to face with truth; to arrive, after innumerable wanderings and pains, at wisdom and bliss; not to be finally defeated and cast out, but ultimately to triumph over every inward foe—such is man's divine destiny, such his glorious goal. And this, every saint, sage, and saviour has declared.

In the present stage of the life of humanity, comparatively few reach this place of triumph—though all will reach it at last—yet there is a glorious company of perfect ones who have attained in the past, and their number is being added to with each succeeding age. Men are as yet learners in the school of life, and most men die learners. But there are some who, in this life, through fixity of purpose and strenuous fighting against darkness, pain, and ignorance, acquire a right knowledge of life and pass joyfully beyond the pupil stage.

Man is not to remain forever a schoolboy in the universe, to be whipped for follies and errors. When he wills and wishes, he can set his mind upon his task and master the lessons of life, becoming a confident and skilled scholar, living in understanding and peace, and not in ignorance and misery.

The sorrows of life are profound and deeply rooted, but they can be fathomed and rooted out. The passions and emotions of human nature are, in their ungoverned state, overwhelming and painfully conflicting, but they can be so softened down, harmonized, and wisely directed and understood, as to become obedient servants for the outworking of enlightened purposes.

The difficulties of life are great, its battle fierce, and its wished-for issues are uncertain and elusive; so much so, that every hour men and women are breaking down under the strain. Yet these conditions have no objective and arbitrary existence. In their true nature they are subjective and purely mental, and can be transcended. There is no inherent and permanent evil in the universal order; and the mind can be lifted up to the moral altitude where evil can touch it no more.

A steadfast faith in an Eternal and Universal Justice, in an over-ruling Good, is the prelude to the Life Triumphant. The man who aims to become strong, serene, and steadfast at heart must, at the onset, have no doubt that the Heart of Life is good. He who is to gaze upon the Cosmic Order and experience the rapture of emancipation must realize that there is no disorder in his life but that which he creates. This realization is difficult, so prone is the mind, in its imperfect stages, to self-pity and self-justification, but it can be attained, and must be attained by him who is to live the freed life. At first it must be believed, and the belief must be adhered to, until it ripens into realization and knowledge.

The sufferings of life are greatly reduced when they are accepted as disciplinary experiences, and the man of faith does so accept them. The sufferings of life are transcended and put away when all experiences are accounted good, and are utilized in the development of character, and the man of knowledge does so regard and utilize them.

Faith is the grey dawn which precedes the full and perfect day of knowledge. Without it there can be no attainment of strength, no permanent security of heart. The man of faith does not succumb when difficulties present themselves; he does not despair when troubles overtake him. However steep and dark his path may seem, he looks forward to a brighter pathway ahead. He sees a destination of rest and light beyond. They who have no faith in the triumph of good ignominiously succumb to the elements of evil. And this must be so; for he who does not elevate good, elevates evil, and, seeing evil as the master of life, he receives the wages of evil.

There are those who, having yielded to defeat in the battle of life, talk thoughtlessly about the wrongs they have suffered at the hands of others. They believe—and try to make others believe—that they would have been successful or rich or famous but for the treachery and villainy of those about them. They tell, for the thousandth time, how they have been deceived, defrauded, and degraded by others. They imagine that they themselves are all trust, all innocence, all honesty and good nature, and that nearly everyone else is all that is bad and malicious. They tell how they would have been just as prosperous and honored as others if they had been as selfish as those others; and that their great drawback, and the chief source, in themselves, of their failures, is that they were born with too great an endowment of unselfishness.

Such self-praising complainers cannot distinguish between good and evil, and their faith in human nature and the goodness of the universe is dead. Looking upon others, they have eyes for evil only; looking upon themselves, they see only suffering innocence. Rather than discover any evil in themselves, they would have all humanity bad. In their hearts they have enthroned the wretched Demon of Evil as the Lord of Life, and see in the course of things only a selfish scramble in which the good is always crushed and the evil rises triumphant. Blind to their own folly, ignorance, and weakness, they see nothing but injustice in their fate, nothing but misery and wretchedness in their present condition.

He who would have even a useful and successful life—yet alone a spiritually noble and victorious one—must at once root out and cast away this wretched condition of mind that negates all that is good and pure, and gives preeminence to all that is base and impure. Misfortune, misery and defeat most surely await the man who believes that dishonesty, deceit and selfishness are the best weapons whereby to achieve a successful life. What courage and strength can a man develop, and what quiet and happiness can he enjoy, who believes that in order to keep pace with others he must continually deny and discourage the better qualities of his nature? The man who believes that evil is more powerful than good, and that bad men have the best of life, is still involved in the elements of evil; and, being so involved, he suffers—must necessarily suffer—defeat.

It may appear to you that the world is given over to wickedness; that the bad prosper, and the good fail; that there is nothing but chance, injustice, and disorder. But do not believe this: regard it as an elusive appearance. Conclude that you do not see life as it really is; that you have not yet fathomed the causes of things, and that when you can look upon life through a purer heart and a wiser mind, you will see and understand its equity. And truly when you do so look at life, you will see good where you now see evil, order where now appears disorder, and justice where now injustice seems to prevail.

The universe is a cosmos, not a chaos, and the bad do not prosper. It is true there is much evil in the world, otherwise there would be no necessity for moral aims, but there is also much misery in the world, and the evil and misery are related as cause and effect. It is equally true that there is much good in the world, and much abiding gladness, and the good and gladness are related as cause and effect. He who has acquired that faith in the power and supremacy of good, which no apparent injustice, no amount of suffering, and no catastrophe can shake, will pass through all emergencies, all trials and difficulties, with a sublime courage that defies the demons of doubt and despair. He may not succeed in all his plans. He may even encounter much failure; but when he fails, it will be that he may frame nobler purposes and ascend to higher achievements. He will only fail in order to reach a success greater than that of which he first dreamed. His life will not, cannot, be a failure. Some of its details will fail, but this will be but the breaking of weak links in the chain of character and events, in order that the whole may be made more strong and complete.

There is an animal courage which can calmly face the fire of an enemy in battle, or the fierce rage of beasts, but which fails in the battle of life and breaks down when confronted with the beasts that rage within one's own heart. It requires a higher, diviner courage to remain calm in the hour of deprivation and calamity than in the heat of battle, to overcome self than to overcome another. And this diviner courage is the companion of faith.

A mere theological belief (commonly confused with faith) will not avail. Beliefs about God, Jesus, Creation, etc., are merely surface opinions (derived chiefly from custom) which do not reach down to the real life of a man and have no power to bestow faith. Such beliefs may accompany faith, but they are distinct from it. Frequently, those who hold most tenaciously to particular beliefs about God, Jesus, and the Bible are most lacking in faith—that is, they give way to complaint, despondency, and grief immediately after some petty trouble overtakes them.

If one is given to irritability, anxiety, hopelessness, and lamentations over the simple things of life, let him know that, in spite of his religious belief or metaphysical philosophy, he lacks faith. For where faith is there is courage, there is fortitude, there is steadfastness and strength.

The opinions of men are lightly to be considered, for they are changing with every new breeze of thought. They have very little part in the reality of things, being the bubbles of a surface effervescence. But behind all opinions there is the same human heart. The "godless" are they who are goodless, even though they may be members of churches and make a great profession of faith in God. The "godly" are they who are goodly even though they make no profession of religion. The complainers and bewailers are the faithless and unbelieving. Those who deny or belittle the power of good, and in their lives and actions affirm and magnify the power of evil, are the only real atheists.

Faith bestows that sublime courage that rises superior to the petty and selfish disappointments and troubles of life, that acknowledges no defeat except as a step to victory; that is strong to endure, patient to wait, and energetic to struggle. It perceives the benign law of Truth in all things, and is assured of the final triumph of the heart, and the kingly power of the mind.

Light up, then, the lamp of faith in your heart, and walk through the darkness guided by its illuminating rays. Its light is dim, and cannot be compared with the sunlight brilliance of knowledge, but it suffices to lead one safely through the mists of doubt and the black darkness of despair; along the narrow, thorny ways of sickness and sorrow, and over the treacherous planes of temptation and uncertainty. It enables man to ward off and outstrip the foul beasts that rage in the jungle of his heart, and to reach safely the open plains of a pure life and the mountain levels of conquest where the dim light of faith is no longer needed. For, leaving behind him all the darkness, all the doubt, error, and sorrow, he enters into a new consciousness and upon a higher round of life, works, and acts, and lives self-contained and peaceful, in the full and glorious light of knowledge.

2
Manliness, Womanliness and Sincerity

Before a man can be truly godly, he must be manly; before a woman can be truly godly, she must be womanly. There can be no true goodness apart from moral strength. Simpering, pretence, artificial behaviour, flatteries, insincerities and smiling hypocrisies—let these things be forever destroyed and banished from our minds. Evil is inherently weak, ineffectual, and cowardly. Good is essentially strong, effective, and courageous. In teaching men and women to be good, I teach them to be strong, free, self-reliant. They will greatly misunderstand me and the principles which I enunciate who imagine that because I teach gentleness, purity, and patience

I teach the cultivation of an effeminate weakness. It is only the manly man and the womanly woman who can properly understand those divine qualities. No one is better equipped to achieve the Life Triumphant than they who, along with active moral qualities and a high sense of purity and honour, are also possessed of the strong animal nature of the normal man.

That animal force which, in various forms, surges within you, and which, in the hour of excitement, carries you blindly away, causing you to forget your higher nature and to forfeit your manly dignity and honour—that same force controlled, mastered, and rightly directed, will endow you with a divine strength by which you can achieve the highest, noblest, most blissful victories of true living.

The savage within you is to be scourged and disciplined into obedience. You are to be the master of your heart, your mind, yourself. Man is only weak and abject when he gives up the reins of government to the lower, instead of directing the lower by the higher. Your passions are to be your servants and slaves, not your masters. See that you keep them in their places, duly controlled and commanded, and they shall render you faithful, strong, and happy service.

You are not "vile." There is no part of your body or mind that is vile. Nature does not make mistakes. The Universe is framed on Truth. All your functions, faculties, and powers are good, and to direct them rightly is wisdom, holiness, happiness; to direct them wrongly is folly, sin, and misery.

Men waste themselves in excesses; in bad tempers, hatreds, gluttonies, and unworthy and unlawful pleasures, and then blame life. They should blame themselves. A man should have more self-respect than to abuse his nature in any way. He should command himself always; should avoid excitement and hurry; should be too noble to give way to anger, to resent the actions and opinions of others, or fruitlessly to argue with an abusive and cantankerous assailant.

A quiet, unobtrusive, and unoffending dignity is the chief mark of a ripe and perfect manhood. Honour others and respect yourself. Choose your own path and walk it with a firm, unflinching step, but avoid a meddlesome interference with others. In the true man opposing qualities are blended and harmonized; a yielding kindness accompanies an unbending strength. He adapts himself gently and wisely to others without sacrificing the steadfast principles upon which his manhood is built. To have that iron strength that can go calmly to death rather than yield one jot of truth, along with that tender sympathy that can shield the weak and mistaken enemy, is to be manly with a divine manhood.

Be true to the dictates of your own conscience, and respect all who do the same, even though their conscience should lead them in a direction the reverse of your own. One of the most unmanly tendencies is to pity another because he chooses opinions or religion contrary to those of one's self. Why pity a man because he is an agnostic, or an atheist, or a Buddhist, or a Christian? Because he does not hold this opinion or that belief? Such pity should be rightly named contempt. It is the office of pity to feel for the weak, the afflicted, and the helpless.

Pity never says "I pity you"; it does kind deeds. It is superciliousness that professes pity for the strong, the self-reliant, for those who have the courage to mark out their own path and to walk it boldly. Why should he be forced to hold my opinion or yours? If what I say and do appeal to his reason and conscience as right, then he will be one with me and will work hand and hand with me. But if my work be not his work, he is nonetheless a man. He has his duty, though it not be my duty. When I meet one who is self-respecting, and who dares to think for himself, I will salute him as a man, and not harbor in my heart a contemptible pity for him, because, indeed, he rejects my conclusions.

If we are to be responsible, self-acting beings in a law-begotten universe, let us be masters of our own wills, and respect the free will of others. If we are to be strong and manly, let us be large-hearted and magnanimous. If we are to triumph over the miseries of life, let us rise superior to the pettiness of our nature.

Men weep in their weakness, and cry out in misery of heart and degradation of mind. How plain, then, is the way of emancipation; how sublime the task of triumph! Be master of yourself. Eliminate weakness. Exorcise the mocking fiend, selfishness, in whom is all weakness and wretchedness. Do not pander to unnatural cravings, to unlawful desires, or to morbid self-love and self-pity. Give them no quarter, but promptly stamp them out with disciplinary decision and strength.

A man should hold himself, as it were, in the hollow of his hand. He should be able to take up and to lay down. He should know how to use things, and not be used by them. He should neither be the helpless captive of luxury nor the whipped slave of want, but should be self-contained and self-sufficient, master of himself under all conditions. He must train and direct his will in the way of self-mastery which is the way of obedience—obedience to the law of his nature. Disobedience to law is the supreme evil in man, the source of all his sin and sorrow. In his ignorance he imagines he can triumph over law and subdue the wills of others. He thus destroys his power.

Man can triumph over his disobedience, over ignorance, sin, egotism, and lawlessness. He can conquer self; and herein lies his manly strength and divine power. He can comprehend the law of his being, and obey it as a child obeys the will of its father. He can sit the crowned king of all his functions and faculties, using them wisely in unselfish service, and not as instruments of selfishness and greed. There is no bad habit that he cannot uproot, no sin that he cannot subdue, no sorrow that he cannot comprehend and conquer. "Let a man then know his worth, and keep things under his feet. Let him not peep or steal, or skulk up and down with the air of a charity boy or an interloper, in the world which exists for him."

A manly self-reliance is not only compatible with, but is the accompaniment of, a divine humility. A man is only arrogant and egotistic when he usurps authority over others. He cannot claim nor exercise too great an authority over himself. Strong self-command, with gentle consideration for others, combine to make the truly manly man.

To begin with, a man must be honest, upright, sincere. Deceit is the blindest folly. Hypocrisy is the weakest thing on earth. In trying to deceive others, a man most of all deceives himself. A man should be so free from guile, meanness, and deceit as to be able to look everybody in the face with a clear, open, unflinching gaze, free from shame and confusion, and with no inward shrinking or misgivings. Without sincerity a man is but a hollow mask, and whatsoever work he attempts to do, it will be lifeless and ineffectual. Out of a hollow vessel nothing but the sound of hollowness can come; and from insincerity nothing but empty words can proceed.

Many are not consciously hypocrites, yet fall victims, thoughtlessly, to little insincerities which undermine happiness and destroy the moral fabric of their character. Some of these people go regularly to their place of worship. They pray daily, year after year, for a purer heart and life, yet come from their devotions to vilify an enemy, or, worse still, to ridicule or slander an absent friend for whom, when they meet him or her, they will have nothing but smiles and smooth words. The pitiful part of it is that they are totally unconscious of their insincerity, and when their friends desert them, they speak complainingly of the faithlessness and hollowness of the world, and of people generally, and tell you sadly that there are no true friends in this world. Truly, for such there are no abiding friendships. For insincerity, even if not seen, is felt, and those who are incapable of bestowing trust and truth, cannot receive it. Be true to others, and others will be true to you. Think well of an enemy, and defend the absent friend. If you have lost faith in human nature, discover where you have gone wrong yourself.

In the Confucian code of morals sincerity is one of the "Five Great Virtues," and Confucius thus speaks of it:

"It is sincerity which places a crown upon your lives. Without it, our best actions would be valueless; the seemingly virtuous, mere hypocrites; and the shining light which dazzles us with its splendour, but a poor passing gleam ready to be extinguished by the slightest breath of passion . . . To be pure in mind, you must be free from self-deception—you must hate vice as you would a disagreeable odour, and love virtue as you would some beautiful object. There can be no self-respect without it, and this is why the superior man must be guarded in his hours of solitude.

"The worthless man secretly employs his idle moments in vicious acts, and there is no limit to his wickedness. In the presence of the pure he plays the hypocrite, and puts forward none but his good qualities. Yet how does this disguise hide him when his true character is revealed to the first scrutinizing glance?

"It has been said that there is a strict watch kept over that which is pointed at by many hands, and gazed at by many eyes. It is in solitude, then, that the upright man has the greatest reason to be guarded."

Thus the sincere man does not do or say that which he would be ashamed of were it brought to light. His uprightness of spirit enables him to walk upright and confident among his fellow men. His presence is a strong protection, and his words are direct and powerful because they are true. Whatever may be his work, it prospers. Though he may not always please the ears of men, he wins their hearts; they rely on him, trust, and honour him.

Courage, self-reliance, sincerity, generosity and kindness—these are the virtues which constitute a robust manhood. Without them, a man is but clay in the hands of circumstances; a weak, wavering thing that cannot rise into the freedom and joy of a true life. Every young man should cultivate and foster these virtues, and as he succeeds in living them will he prepare to achieve the Life Triumphant.

I see coming upon the earth a new race of men and women—men who will be men indeed, strong, upright, noble; too wise to stoop to anger, uncleanness, strife, and hatred—women who would be women indeed, gentle, truthful, pure; too compassionate to stoop to gossip, slander, and deception. From their loins will proceed superior beings of the same noble type; and the dark fiends of error and evil will fall back at their approach. These noble men and women will regenerate the earth. They will dignify man, and vindicate nature, restoring humanity to love, happiness, and peace; and the life of victory over sin and sorrow will be established in the earth.

3

Energy and Power

How wonderful is the universal energy! Never-tiring, inexhaustible, and apparently eternal in its operation, it moves in atom and in star, informing the fleeting shapes of tune with its restless, glowing, pulsating power.

Man is a portion of this creative energy, and in him it manifests, through a combination of mental faculties, as affection, passion, intelligence, morality, reason, understanding, and wisdom. He is not merely a blind conductor of energy, but he consciously uses, controls, and directs it. Slowly, but with certainty, is he gaining control of the forces without, and is making them do obedient service. And just as surely will he gain control of the forces within—the subtle energies of thought—and direct them into channels of harmony and happiness.

Man's true place in the Cosmos is that of a king, not a slave, a commander under the law of Good and not a helpless tool in the reign of Evil. His own body and mind are the dual dominion over which he is to reign, a Lord of Truth, the master of himself, the wise user and controller of his store of pure, eternal, creative energy. Let him walk the earth unashamed, strong, valiant, tender, and kind; no longer prostrate in self-abasement, but walking erect in the dignity of perfect manhood; not groveling in selfishness and remorse, nor crying for pardon and mercy, but standing firm and free in the sublime majesty of a sinless life.

Long has man regarded himself as vile, weak, and unworthy, and has been content to remain so. But in the new era which has just now burst upon the world, he is to make a glorious discovery that he is pure, powerful, and noble when he rises up and wills. The rising up is not against any outward enemy; not against neighbour, nor governments, nor laws, nor spirits, nor principalities, but against the ignorance, folly, and misery which beset him in the dominion of his own mind. For it is only by ignorance and folly that man is slavish; by knowledge and wisdom his kingdom is restored.

Let them who will, preach man's weakness and helplessness, but I will teach his strength and power. I write for men, not for babes; for those who are eager to learn, and earnest to achieve; for those who will put away (for the world's good) a petty personal indulgence, a selfish desire, a mean thought, and live on as though it were not, without craving and regret. The Truth is not for the frivolous and the thoughtless. The Life Triumphant is not for triflers and loiterers.

Man is a master. If he were not, he could not act contrary to law. Thus his so-called weakness is an indication of strength; his sin is the inversion of his capacity for holiness. For what is his weakness and sin but misdirected energy, misapplied power? In this sense, the wrongdoer is strong, not weak; but he is ignorant, and exerts his strength in wrong directions instead of right, against the law of things instead of with it.

Suffering is the recoil of misdirected strength, The bad man becomes good by reversing his conduct. If you are weeping over your sins, cease to commit those sins and establish yourself in their opposing virtues. It is thus that weakness is converted into strength, helplessness into power, and suffering into bliss. By turning his energies from the old channels of vice, and directing them into the new channels of virtue, the sinner becomes a saint.

While the universal energy may be unlimited, in particular forms its sum is strictly limited. A man is possessed of a given amount of energy, and he can use it or misuse it, can conserve and concentrate it, or dissipate and disperse it. Power is concentrated energy; wisdom is that energy adapted to beneficent ends. He is the man of influence and power who directs all his energies towards one great purpose, and patiently works and waits for its fulfilment, sacrificing his desires in other and more pleasant directions. He is the man of folly and weakness who, thinking chiefly of pleasure, gratifies the desire of the hour, or follows the whim and impulse of the moment, and so drifts thoughtlessly into peevishness and poverty of mind.

The energy used in one direction is not available for use in other directions; this is a universal law both in mind and matter. Emerson calls it "the law of compensation." Gain in a given direction necessitates loss in its opposite direction. The force placed in one scale is deducted from the other scale. Nature is always endeavoring to strike a balance. The energy which is dissipated in idleness is not given to work. The pleasure-seeker cannot also be a Truth-seeker.

The force wasted in a fit of bad temper is drawn from the man's store of virtue, particularly the virtue of patience. Spiritually, this law of compensation is the law of sacrifice. Selfish pleasure must be sacrificed if purity is to be gained; hatred must be yielded up if love is to be acquired; vice must be renounced if virtue is to be embraced.

Earnest men soon discover that if they are to accomplish anything that is successful, strong, and enduring, in worldly, intellectual, or spiritual channels, they must curb their desires, and sacrifice much that seems sweet; yea, even much that seems important.

Hobbies, bodily and mental indulgences, enticing companionships, alluring pleasures, and all work that does not tend to some central purpose in his life must be sacrificed by the man of strong resolve. He opens his eyes to the fact that time and energy are strictly limited, and so he economizes the one and concentrates the other.

Foolish men waste their energies in swinish ease and gluttonous indulgence, in frivolous pleasures and empty talk, in hateful thoughts and irritable outbursts of passion, in vain controversy and meddlesome interference. They then complain that many are more "fortunately equipped than they are for a useful, successful, or great life, and they envy their honoured neighbour who has sacrificed self to duty, and has devoted all his energies to the faithful performance of the business of his life.

"He who is just, speaks the truth, and does what is his own business, him the world will hold dear." Let a man attend to his own business, concentrating all his energies upon the perfect accomplishment of the task of his life, not stepping aside to condemn or interfere with the duties of others, and he will find life simple, strong, and happy.

The universe is girt with goodness and strength, and it protects the strong and the good. Evil and weakness are self-destructive. Dissipation is annihilation. All nature loves strength. I see no inherent cruelty in "the survival of the fittest." It is a spiritual as well as a natural law. The stronger qualities of the beast are the fittest to evolve a higher type. The nobler moral qualities in man are his emancipators, and it is well that they should dominate and ultimately crush out the ignoble tendencies.

Most certain it is that he who gives dominion to the lower, courts destruction, and does not survive, either in the struggle of life without or the battle of Truth within. The life given to the lower is lost to the higher; yea, it is finally lost also to the lower, and so all is lost, for evil is ultimately nothingness. But the life given to the higher is preserved, and is not lost to anything, for, while it sacrifices much that the world holds precious, it does not sacrifice anything that is precious in reality.

The untrue and worthless must perish, and he who consecrates himself to the good and the true is content that they should perish, and so at last he stands where sacrifice ends, and all is gain—such a one survives in the struggle of life without, and he conquers in the battle of Truth within.

First, then, be strong. Strength is the firm basis on which is built the temple of the Triumphant Life.

Without a central motive and fixed resolve, your life will be a poor, weak, drifting, unstable thing. Let the act of the moment be governed by the deep abiding purpose of the heart. You will act differently at different times, but the act will not be wrong if the heart is right. You may fall and go astray at times, especially under great stress, but you will quickly regain yourself, and you will grow wiser and stronger, thereby, so long as you guide yourself by the moral compass within, and do not throw it away to gratify indulgence and give yourself up to uncertain drifting.

Follow your conscience. Be true to your convictions. Do at the moment what you regard as right, and put away all procrastination, vacillation, and fear. If you are convinced that in the performance of your duty under certain circumstances the severest measures are necessary, carry out those measures, and let there be no uncertainty about it. Err on the side of strength rather than weakness. The measures you adopt may not be the best, but if they are the best you know, then your plain duty is to carry them out. By so doing you will discover the better way, if you are anxious for progress, and are willing to learn. Deliberate beforehand, but in the tune of action do not hesitate.

Avoid anger and stubbornness, lust and greed. The angry man is the weak man. The stubborn man, who refuses to learn or mend his ways, is the foolish man. He grows old in folly, and grey hairs do not bring him reverence or honour. The sensualist has energy for pleasure only, and reserves none for manliness and self-respect. The greedy man is blind to the nobility of human nature and the glory of a true life; he spends his energies in perpetuating the miseries of hell, instead of enjoying the happiness of heaven.

Your strength is with you, and you can spend it in burrowing downward or in climbing upward. You can dissipate it in selfishness or conserve it in goodness. The same energy will enable you to become a beast or a god. The course along which you direct it will determine its effect. Do not think the thought, "My mind is weak," but convert weakness into strength, and energy into power by redirecting your mental forces. Turn your thoughts into noble channels. Put away vain longings and foolish regrets; abolish complaint and self-condolence, and have no dalliance with evil. Lift your face upward. Rise up in your divine strength, and spurn from your mind and life all meanness and weakness. Do not live the false life of a whining slave, but live the true life of a conquering master.

4

Self-Control and Happiness

When mental energy is allowed to follow the line of least resistance, and to fall into easy channels, it is called weakness. When it is gathered, focused, and forced into upward and different directions, it becomes power; and this concentration of energy and acquisition of power is brought about by means of self-control.

In speaking of self-control, one is easily misunderstood. It should not be associated with a destructive repression, but with a constructive expression. The process is not one of death, but of life. It is a divine and masterly transmutation in which the weak is converted into the strong, the coarse into the fine, and the base into the noble; in which virtue takes the place of vice, and dark passion is lost in bright intellectuality.

The man who merely smothers up and hides away his real nature, without any higher object in view than to create a good impression upon others concerning his character, is practicing hypocrisy and not self-control. As the mechanic transmutes coal into gas, and water into steam, and then concentrates and utilizes the finer forces for the comfort and convenience of others, so the man who intellectually practices self-control transmutes his lower inclinations into the finer qualities of intelligence and mortality to the increase of his own and the world's happiness.

A man is happy, wise, and great in the measure that he controls himself; he is wretched, foolish, and mean in the measure that he allows his animal nature to dominate his thoughts and actions.

He who controls himself controls his life, his circumstances, his destiny, and wherever he goes he carries his happiness with him as an abiding possession. He who does not control himself, is controlled by passions, by his circumstances, and his fate; and if he cannot gratify the desire of the moment, he is disappointed and miserable. He depends for his fitful happiness on external things.

There is no force in the universe which can be annihilated or lost. Energy is transformed, but not destroyed. To shut the door on old and bad habits is to open it to new and better ones. Renunciation precedes regeneration. Every self-indulgence, every forbidden pleasure, every hateful thought renounced is transformed into something more purely and permanently beautiful. Where debilitating excitements are cut off, there spring up rejuvenating joys. The seed dies that the flower may appear; the grub perishes, but the dragonfly comes forth.

Truly, the transformation is not instantaneous; nor is the transition a pleasant and painless process. Nature demands effort and patience as the price of growth. In the march of progress, every victory is contested with struggle and pain; but the victory is achieved, and it abides. The struggle passes; the pain is temporary only. To demolish a firmly fixed habit, to break up a mental tendency that has become automatic with long use, and to force into birth and growth a fine characteristic or lofty virtue—to accomplish this necessitates a painful metamorphosis, a transitional period of darkness, to pass through which patience and endurance are required.

This is where men fail. This is where they slip back into their old, easy, animal ruts, and abandon self-control as too strenuous and severe. Thus they fall short of permanent happiness, and the life of triumph over evil is hidden from their eyes.

The permanent happiness which men seek in dissipation, excitement, and abandonment to unworthy pleasure is found only in the life which reverses all this—the life of self-control. So far as a man deviates from perfect self-command, just so far does he fall short of perfect happiness. He sinks into misery and weakness, the lowest limit of which is madness, entire lack of mental control, the condition of irresponsibility. In so far as a man approximates to perfect self-command, just so near does he approach to perfect happiness, and rise into joy and strength. So glorious are the possiblities of such divine manhood, that no limit can be set to its grandeur and bliss.

If a man will understand how intimately, yea, how inseparably, self-control and happiness are associated, he has but to look into his own heart, and upon the world around, to find there the joy destroying effects of uncontrolled tendencies. Looking upon the lives of men and women, he will perceive how the hasty word, the bitter retort, the act of deception, the blind prejudice and foolish resentment bring wretchedness and even ruin in their train. Looking into his own life, what days of consuming remorse, of restless anxiety, and of crushing sorrow rise up before his mind—periods of intense suffering through which he has passed through lack of self-control.

But in the right life, the well-governed life, the victorious life, all these things pass away. New conditions obtain, and purer, more spiritual instruments are employed for the achievements of happy ends. There is no more remorse, because there is no more wrong-doing. There is no more anxiety, because there is no more selfishness. There is no more sorrow, because Truth is the source of action.

The much desired thing which self pursues with breathless and uncontrolled eagerness, yet fails to overtake, comes unbidden, and begs to be admitted, to him who works and waits in perfect self-command. Hatred, impatience, greed, self-indulgence, vain ambitions, and blind desires—the instruments by which self shapes its ill-finished existence, what clumsy tools they are, and how ignorant and unskilful are they who employ them! Love, patience, kindness, self-discipline, transmuted ambitions, and chastened desires—instruments of Truth, by which is shaped a wellfinished existence, what perfect tools they are, and how wise and skilful are they who use them!

Whatsoever is gained by feverish haste and selfish desire is attained in fuller measure by quietness and renunciation. Nature will not be hastened. She brings all perfection in due season. Truth will not be commanded. He has his conditions and must be obeyed. Nothing is more superfluous than haste and anger.

A man has to learn he cannot command things, but that he can command himself; that he cannot coerce the wills of others, but that he can mold and master his own will: and things serve him who serve Truth. People seek guidance of him who is master of himself.

It is a little understood, yet simple and profound truth, that the man who cannot command himself under the severest external stress is unfit to guide others or to control affairs. It is the fundamental principle in the moral and political teachings of Confucius that, before attempting to govern affairs, a man should learn to govern himself. Men who habitually give way, under pressure, to hysterical suspicions, outbursts of resentment, and explosions of anger, are unfit for weighty responsibilities and lofty duties, and usually fail, sooner or later, even in the ordinary duties of life, such as the management of their own family or business. Lack of self-control is foolishness, and folly cannot take precedence over wisdom. He who is learning how to subdue and control his turbulent, wandering thoughts is becoming wiser every day. Though for a time the Temple of Joy will not be completed, he will gather strength in laying its foundations and building its walls; and the day will come when, like a wise masterbuilder, he will rest at peace in the beautiful habitation which he has built. Wisdom inheres in self-control and in wisdom is "pleasantness and peace."

The life of self-control is no barren deprivation, no wilderness of monotony. Renunciation there is, but it is a renunciation of the ephemeral and false in order that the abiding and true may be realized. Enjoyment is not cut off; it is intensified. Enjoyment is life; it is the slavish desire for it that kills. Is there anywhere a more miserable man than he who is always longing for some new sensation? Is there anywhere a more blessed being than he who, by self-control, is satisfied, calm, and enlightened? Who has most of physical life and joy—the glutton, the drunkard, and the sensualist who lives for pleasure only, or the temperate man who holds his body in subjection, considering its needs and obeying its uses?

I was once eating a ripe, juicy apple as it came from the tree, and a man near me said, "I would give anything if I could enjoy an apple like that." I asked, "Why can't you?" His answer was, "I have drunk whiskey and smoked tobacco until I have lost all enjoyment in such things." In pursuit of elusive enjoyments, men lose the abiding joys of life.

And as he who controls his senses has most of physical life, joy, and strength, so he who controls his thoughts has most of spiritual life, bliss, and power. For not only happiness, but knowledge and wisdom also are revealed by self-control. As the avenues of ignorance and selfishness are closed, the open gates of knowledge and enlightenment appear. Virtue attained is knowledge gained. The pure mind is an enlightened mind. He has well-being who controls himself well.

I hear men speak of the "monotony of goodness." If looking for things in the spirit which one has given up in the letter were "goodness," then indeed would it be monotonous. The man of self-control does not merely give up his base pleasures, he abandons all longing for them. He presses forward, and does not look back; and fresh beauties, new glories, sublimer vistas await him at every step.

I am astonished at the revelations which lie hidden in self-control; I am captivated by the infinite variety of Truth, I am filled with joy at the grandeur of the prospect; I am gladdened by its splendour and its peace.

Along the way of self-control there is the joy of victory; the consciousness of expanding and increasing power; the acquisition of the imperishable riches of divine knowledge; and the abiding bliss of service to humankind. Even he who travels only a portion of the way will develop a strength, achieve a success, and experience a joy which the idle and the thoughtless cannot know. And he who goes all the way will become a spiritual conqueror; he will triumph over all evil, and will blot it out. He will gaze with enrapt vision upon the majesty of the Cosmic Order, and will enjoy the immortality of Truth.

5
Simplicity and Freedom

You have known what it is to be physically encumbered by some superfluous load. You have experienced the happy relief of dispensing with such a load. Your experience illustrates the difference between a life burdened with a complexity of desires, beliefs, and speculations, and one rendered simple and free by the satisfaction of its natural needs, and a calm contemplation of the facts of existence, eliminating all argument and speculation.

There are those who cumber their drawers, cupboards, and rooms with rubbish and clutter. To such an extent is this carried sometimes, that the house cannot be properly cleaned, and vermin swarms. There is no use for the rubbish, but they will not part with it, even though by so doing, they would also get rid of the vermin. But they like to think that it is there; like to feel that they have got it, especially if they are convinced that nobody else has its like. They reason that it may be of some use someday; or it may become valuable; or it brings up old associations which they occasionally resuscitate and take a paradoxical pleasure in sorrowing over.

In a sweet, methodical, well-managed house, such superfluities, bringing with them dirt, discomfort, and care, are not allowed to accumulate. Or should they have accumulated, they are gathered up and consigned to the fire and the trash bin, when it is decided to cleanse and restore the house, and give it light, comfort, and freedom.

In a like manner men hoard up in their minds mental rubbish and clutter, cling tenaciously to it, and fear its loss. Insatiate desires; thirsty cravings for unlawful and unnatural pleasures; conflicting beliefs about miracles, gods, angels, demons, and interminable theological complexities, hypothesis is piled upon hypothesis, speculation is added to speculation, until the simple, beautiful, all-sufficient facts of life are lost to sight and knowledge beneath the metaphysical pile.

Simplicity consists in being rid of this painful confusion of desires and superfluity of opinions, and adhering only to that which is permanent and essential. And what is permanent in life? What is essential? Virtue alone is permanent; character is essential. So simple is life when it is freed from all superfluities and rightly understood and lived that it can be reduced to a few unmistakable, easy-tounderstand, though hard-to-practice principles. And all great minds have so simplified life.

Buddha reduced it to eight virtues, in the practice of which he declared that men would acquire perfect enlightenment. And these eight virtues he reduced to one, which he called compassion.

Confucius taught that the perfection of knowledge was contained in five virtues, and these he expressed in one which he called Reciprocity, or Sympathy.

Jesus reduced the whole of life to the principle of Love. Compassion, Sympathy, Love, these three are identical. How simple they are, too! Yet I cannot find a man who fully understands the depths and heights of these virtues, for who so fully understood them would embody them in practice. He would be complete, perfect, divine. There would be nothing lacking in him of knowledge, virtue, and wisdom.

It is only when a man sets earnestly to work to order his life in accordance with the simple precepts of virtue, that he discovers what piles of mental rubbish he has hoarded up, and which he is now compelled to throw away. The exactions, too, which such a course of conduct make upon his faith, endurance, patience, kindness, humility, reason, and strength of will, are, until the mind approaches the necessary condition of purity and simplicity, painful in their severity. The clearing-out process, whether of one's mind, home, or place of business, is not a light and easy one, but it ends in comfort and repose.

All complexities of detail, whether in things material or mental, are reducible to a few fundamental laws or principles by virtue of which they exist and are regulated. Wise men govern their lives by a few simple rules. A life governed by the central principle of love will be found to be divinely consistent in all its details. Every thought, word, act, will fall into proper place, and there will be no conflict and confusion.

"What," asked the learned man of the Buddhist saint who had acquired a wide reputation for sanctity and wisdom—"is the most fundamental thing in Buddhism?" The saint replied, "The most fundamental thing in Buddhism is to cease from evil and to learn to do good." "I did not ask you," said the learned man, "to tell me what every child of three knows. I want you to tell me what is the most profound, the most subtle, and the most important thing in Buddhism." "The most profound, the most subtle, the most important thing in Buddhism," said the saint, "is to cease from evil and to learn to do well. It is true that a child of three may know it, but grey-haired old men fail to put it into practice."

The commentator then goes on to say that the learned man did not want facts; he did not want Truth. He wanted to be given some subtle metaphysical speculation which would give rise to another speculation, and then to another and another, and so afford him an opportunity of bringing into play the wonderful intellect of which he was so proud.

A member of a philosophical school once proudly said to me, "Our system of metaphysics is the most perfect and the most complicated in the world." I discovered how complicated it was by becoming involved in it and then pursuing the process of disentanglement back to the facts of life, simplicity, and freedom.

I have since learned how better to utilize my energy and occupy my time in the pursuit and practice of those virtues that are firm and sure, rather than to waste it in the spinning of the pretty but unsubstantial threads of metaphysical cobwebs.

But while regarding with disfavour assumption and pride, and that vanity which mistakes its own hypothesis for reality, I set no premium on ignorance and stupidity. Learning is a good thing. As an end in itself, as a possession to be proud of, it is a dead thing; but as a means to the high ends of human progress and human good it becomes a living power. Accompanied with a lowly mind, it is a powerful instrument for good.

The Buddhist saint was no less learned than his proud questioner, but he was more simple and wise. Even hypotheses will not lead us astray if they are perceived as mere hypotheses and are not confounded with facts. Yet the wisest men dispense with all hypotheses, and fall back on the simple practice of virtue. They thus become divine, and arrive at the acme of simplicity, enlightenment, and emancipation.

To arrive at the freedom and joy of simplicity, one must not think less, he must think more; only the thinking must be set to a high and useful purpose, and must be concentrated upon the facts and duties of life, instead of dissipated in unprofitable theorizing.

A life of simplicity is simple in all its parts because the heart which governs it has become pure and strong; because it is centred and rested in Truth. Harmful luxuries in food and vain superfluities in dress; exaggerations of speech and insincerities of action; thoughts that tend to intellectual display and empty speculation—all these are set aside in order that virtue may be better understood and more earnestly embraced. The duties of life are undertaken in a spirit from which self is eliminated, and they become transfigured with a new and glorious light, even the light of Truth. The great fundamental facts of life, heretofore hidden from knowledge, are plainly revealed, and the Eternal Verities, about which the wordy theorizers can only guess and argue, become substantial possessions.

The simple-hearted, the true-hearted, the virtuous and wise, are no longer troubled with doubts and fears about the future and the unknown and unknowable. They take their stand upon the duty of the hour, and on the known and the knowable. They do not barter away the actual for the hypothetical.

They find in virtue an abiding security. They find in Truth an illuminating light which, while it reveals to them the true order of the facts of life, throws a halo of divine promise about the abyss of the unknown; and so they are at rest.

Simplicity works untrammelled, and becomes greatness and power. Suspicions, deceptions, impurities, despondencies, bewailings, doubts, and fears—all these are cast away, left behind and ignored, and the freed man, strong, self-possessed, calm, and pure, works in unclouded assurance, and inhabits heavenly planes.

6

Right Thinking and Repose

Life is a combination of habits, some baneful, some beneficent, all of which take their rise in the one habit of thinking. The thought makes the man; therefore right-thinking is the most important thing in life. The essential difference between a wise man and a fool is that the wise man controls his thinking, the fool is controlled by it. A wise man determines how and what he shall think, and does not allow external things to divert his thought from the main purpose. But a fool is carried captive by every tyrant thought as it is aroused within him by external things, and he goes through life the helpless tool of impulse, whim, and passion.

Careless, slovenly thinking, commonly called thoughtlessness, is the companion of failure, wrongdoing, and wretchedness. Nothing, no prayers, no religious ceremonies, not even acts of charity, can make up for wrong-thinking. Only right-thinking can rectify a wrong life. Only the right attitude of mind towards men and things can bring repose and peace.

The Triumphant Life is only for him whose heart and intellect are attuned to lofty virtue. He must make his thought logical, sequential, harmonious, symmetrical. He must mold and shape his thinking to fixed principles, and thereby establish his life on the sure foundation of knowledge. He must not merely be kind, he must be intelligently kind; must know why he is kind. His kindness must be an invariable quality, and not an intermittent impulse interspersed with fits of resentment and acts of harshness. He must not merely be virtuous under virtuous circumstances; his virtue must be of a kind that shall continue to shine with unabated light when he is assailed with vicious circumstances. He must not allow himself to be hurled from the throne of divine manhood by the shocks of fate or the praise and blame of those around him. Virtue must be his abiding habitation; his refuge from the whirlwind and the storm.

And virtue is not only of the heart; it is of the intellect also; and without this virtue of the intellect, the virtue of the heart is imperiled. Reason, like passion, has its vices. Metaphysical speculations are the riot of the intellect, as sensuality is the riot of the affections. The highest flights of speculation—pleasing as they are—reveal no place of rest, and the strained mind must return to facts and moral principles to find that truth which it seeks. As the soaring bird returns for refuge and rest to its nest in the rock, so must the speculative thinker return to the rock of virtue for surety and peace.

The intellect must be trained to comprehend the principles of virtue, and to understand all that is involved in their practice. Its energies must be restrained from wasteful indulgence in vain subtleties, and be directed in the path of righteousness and the way of wisdom. The thinker must distinguish, in his own mind, between reality and assumption. He must discover the extent of his actual knowledge. He must know what he knows. He must also know what he does not know. He must learn to discriminate between belief and knowledge, error and Truth.

In his search for the right attitude of mind which perceives truth, and works out a wise and radiant life, he must be more logical than logic, more merciless in exposing the errors of his own mind than the most sarcastic logician is in exposing the errors of the minds of others. After pursuing this course of discrimination for a short time, he will be astonished to find how small is the extent of his actual knowledge; yet he will be gladdened by its possession, for small as it is, it is the pure gold of knowledge. And what is better, to have a few grains of gold hidden away in tons of ore, where it is useless, or to extract the gold and throw away the ore?

As the miner sifts away bushels of dull earth to find the sparkling diamond, so the spiritual miner, the true thinker, sifts away from his mind the accumulation of opinions, beliefs, speculations, and assumptions to find the bright jewel of Truth which bestows upon its possessor wisdom and enlightenment.

And the concentrated knowledge which is ultimately brought to light by this sifting process is found to be so closely akin to virtue that it cannot be divided from it, cannot be set apart as something different.

In his search for knowledge Socrates discovered virtue. The divine maxims of the Great Teachers are maxims of virtue. When knowledge is separated from virtue, wisdom is lost. What a man practices, that he knows. What he does not practice, that he does not know. A man may write treatises or preach sermons on Love, but if he treats his family harshly, or thinks spitefully of his enemy, what knowledge has he concerning Love?

In the heart of the man of knowledge there dwells a silent and abiding compassion that shames the fine words of the noisy theorist. He only knows what peace is whose heart is free from hatred, who lives in peace with all. Cunning definitions of virtue only serve to deepen ignorance when they proceed from vice-stained lips. Knowledge has a deeper source than the mere memorizing of information. That knowledge is divine which proceeds from acquaintance with virtue. The humility which purges the intellect of its empty opinions and vain assumptions also fortifies it with a searching insight and invincible power. There is a divine logic which is indistinguished from love. The reply, "He that is without sin among you, let him cast the first stone," is unanswerable logic. It is also perfect love.

The wrong thinker is known by his vices; the right thinker is know by his virtues. Troubles and unrest assail the mind of the wrong thinker, and he experiences no abiding repose. He imagines that others can injure, snub, cheat, degrade and ruin him. Knowing nothing of the protection of virtue, he seeks the protection of self, and takes refuge in suspicion, spite, resentment, and retaliation, and is burnt in the fire of his own vices.

When slandered, he slanders in return; when accused, he recriminates; when assailed, he turns upon his adversary with double fierceness. "I have been treated unjustly!" exclaims the wrong thinker, and then abandons himself to resentment and misery. Having no insight and unable to distinguish evil from good, he cannot see that his own evil, and not his neighbour's, is the cause of all his trouble.

The right thinker is not concerned with thoughts about self and self-protection, and the wrong actions of others towards him cannot cause him trouble or unrest. He cannot think—"This man has wronged me." He perceives that no wrong can reach him but by his own evil deeds. He understands that his welfare is at his own hands, and thus none but himself can rob him of repose. Virtue is his protection, and retaliation is foreign to him. He holds himself steadfastly in peace, and resentment cannot enter his heart. Temptation does not find him unprepared, and it assails in vain the strong citadel of his mind. Abiding in virtue, he abides in strength and peace.

The right-thinker has discovered and acquired the right attitude of mind toward men and things—the attitude of a profound and loving repose. And this is not resignation, it is wisdom. It is not indifference, but watchful and penetrating insight. He has comprehended the facts of life; he sees things as they are. He does not overlook the particulars of life, but reads them in the light of cosmic law; sees them in their right relations as portions of the universal scheme. He sees the universe is upheld by justice. He watches, but does not engage in, the petty quarrels and fleeting strifes of men. He cannot be partisan. His sympathy is with all. He cannot favour one portion more than another. He knows that good will ultimately conquer in the world, as it has conquered in individuals; that there is a sense in which good already conquers, for evil defeats itself.

Good is not defeated; justice is not set aside. Whatever man may do, justice reigns, and its eternal throne cannot be assailed and threatened, much less conquered and overthrown. This is the source of the true thinker's abiding repose. Having become righteous, he perceives the righteous law. Having acquired Love, he understands the Eternal Love. Having conquered evil, he knows that good is supreme.

He is only the true thinker whose heart is free from hatred, lust, and pride; who looks out upon the world through eyes washed free from evil; whose bitterest enemy arouses no enmity, but only tender pity in his heart; who does not talk vainly about things of which he has no knowledge, and whose heart is always at peace.

And by this a man may know that his thoughts are in accordance with the Truth—that there is no more bitterness in his heart, that malice has departed from him; that he loves where he formerly condemned.

A man may be learned, but if he is not wise he will not be a true thinker. Not by learning will a man triumph over evil; not by much study will he overcome sin and sorrow. Only by conquering himself will he conquer evil; only by practicing righteousness will he put an end to sorrow.

Not for the clever, nor the learned, nor the self-confident is the Life Triumphant, but for the pure, the virtuous, the wise. The former achieve their particular success in life, but the latter alone achieve the Great Success, a success so invincible and complete that even an apparent defeat shines with added victory.

Virtue cannot be shaken; virtue cannot be confounded; virtue cannot be overthrown. He who thinks in accordance with virtue, who acts righteously, whose mind is the servant of truth, he it is who conquers in life and in death. For virtue must triumph, and Righteousness and Truth are the pillars of the universe.

7
Calmness and Resource

He who has truth is always self-possessed. Hurry and excitement, anxiety and fear have no place in the purified mind and the true life. Self-conquest results in perpetual calm. Calmness is the radiant light which adds a lustre to all the virtues. Like the nimbus round the head of the saint, it surrounds virtue with its shining halo. Without calmness a man's greatest strength is but a kind of exaggerated weakness. Where is a man's spiritual strength—where indeed, is his ordinary manly strength—who loses his balance with almost every petty disturbance from without? And what enduring influence can a man have who forgets himself in sinful abandonment or unseemly rage in the hour of temptation and crisis?

The virtuous put a check upon themselves, and set a watch upon their passions and emotions. In this way they gain possession of the mind, and gradually acquire calmness. And as they acquire calmness, they acquire influence, power, greatness, abiding joy, and fullness and completeness of life.

Those who do not put a check upon themselves, whose emotions and passions are their masters, who crave excitement and race after unholy pleasures— these are not yet fit for a life of joyful victory, and can neither appreciate nor receive the beautiful jewel of calmness. Such may pray for peace with their lips, but they do not desire it in their hearts; or the word "peace" may only mean to them another kind of periodic pleasure which they desire to enjoy.

In the life of calm there are no fitful periods of sinful excitement followed by reactionary hours of sorrow and remorse. There are no foolish elations followed by equally foolish depressions; no degrading actions followed by misery and loss of self-respect. All these things are put away, and what remains is Truth, and Truth is forever encircled with peace. The calm life is new unbroken bliss. Duties which are irksome to the ungoverned are things of joy to the calm man. Indeed, in the calm life, the word "duty" receives a new meaning. It is no longer opposed to happiness, but it is one with happiness. The calm man, the right-seeing man, cannot separate joy from duty. Such separation belongs to the mind and life of the pleasure-hunter and lover of excitement.

Calmness is difficult to attain because men cling blindly to the lower disturbances of the mind for the passing pleasure which these disturbances afford. Even sorrow is sometimes selfishly gloated over as a kind of occasional luxury. But though difficult to attain, the way which leads to its attainment is simple. It consists of abandoning all those excitements and disturbances which are opposed to it, and fortifying one's self in these steadfast virtues, which do not change with changing events and circumstances, which have no violent reactions, and which therefore bestow perpetual satisfaction and abiding peace.

He only finds peace who conquers himself, who strives, day by day, after self-possession, greater self-control, greater calmness of mind. One can only be a joy to himself and a blessing to others in the measure that he has command of himself; and such self-command is gained only by persistent practice. A man must conquer his weaknesses by daily effort. He must understand them and study how to eliminate them from his character. If he continues to strive, not giving way, he will gradually become victorious. Each little victory gained (though there is a sense in which no victory can be called little) will be so much more calmness acquired and added to his character as an eternal possession.

He will thus make himself strong, capable, and blessed, fit to perform his duties faultlessly, and to meet all events with an untroubled spirit. But even if he does not, in this life, reach that supreme calm which no shock can disturb, he will become sufficiently self-possessed and pure to enable him to fight the battle of life fearlessly, and to leave the world a little richer for having known the goodness of his presence.

By constantly overcoming self, a man gains a knowledge of the subtle intricacies of his mind; and it is this divine knowledge which enables him to become established in calmness. Without self-knowledge there can be no abiding peace of mind, and those who are carried away by tempestuous passions cannot approach the holy place where calmness reigns. The weak man is like one who, having mounted a fiery steed, allows it to run away with him, and carry him withersoever it wills. The strong man is like one who, having mounted the steed, governs it with a masterly hand, and makes it go in whatever direction, and at whatever speed he commands.

Calmness is the crowning beauty of a character that has become, or is becoming, divine, and is restful and peace-giving to all who come in contact with it. Those who are still in their weakness and doubt, find the presence of the calm mind restful to their troubled minds, inspiring to their faltering feet, and rich with healing and comfort in the hour of sorrow. For he who is strong to overcome self is strong to help others. He who has conquered soul-weariness is strong to help the weary on the way. That calmness of mind, which is not disturbed or overthrown by trials and emergencies, or by the accusations, slanders, and misrepresentations of others, is born of great spiritual strength. It is the true indication of an enlightened and wise understanding. The calm mind is the exalted mind. Divinely gentle and externally strong is that man who does not lose his serenity, nor forget his peace when falsehoods and indignities are heaped upon him. Such calmness is the perfect flower of self-control. It has been slowly and laboriously gained, by patiently passing through the fires of suffering, by subjecting the mind to a long process of purification.

The calm man has discovered the spring of both happiness and knowledge within himself, and it is a spring than can never run dry. His powers are at his full command, and there is no limit to his resources. In whatever direction he employs his energies, he will manifest originality and power. And this is so because he deals with things as they are, and not with mere opinions about things, If he has any opinions left, he is no longer enamored of them, but sees them as they are—mere opinions, and therefore of no intrinsic value. He has abolished egotism, and, by obedience to law, has become one with the power in nature and the universe. His resources are untrammeled by selfishness; his energies unhindered by pride.

There is a sense in which he has ceased to regard anything as his own. Even his virtues belong to Truth, and not exclusively to his person. He has become a conscious principle of Cosmic Power, and is no longer a mean, dwarfed thing, seeking petty personal ends. And having put away self, he has put away the greed, the misery, the troubles and fears which belong to self. He acts calmly, and accepts all consequences with equal calmness. He is efficient and accurate, and perceives all that is involved in any undertaking. He does not work blindly; he knows that there is no chance of favour.

The mind of the calm man is like the surface of a still lake; it reflects life and the things of life truly. Whereas, the troubled mind, like the troubled surface of the lake, gives back a distorted image of all things which fall upon it. Gazing into the serene depths within him, the self-conquered man sees a just reflection of the universe. He sees the Cosmic Perfection; sees the equity in his own lot. Even those things which are regarded by the world as unjust and grievous (and which formerly appeared so to him) are now known to be the effects of his own past deeds, and are therefore joyfully accepted as portions of the perfect whole. Thus his calmness remains with him with its illimitable fund of resource in joy and enlightenment.

The calm man succeeds where the disturbed man fails. He is fit to deal with any external difficulty, who has successfully grappled with the most intricate difficulties and problems within his own heart. He who has succeeded in governing the within is best equipped to govern the without. The calm mind perceives a difficulty in all its bearings and understands best how to meet it. The disturbed mind is the lost mind. It has become blind, seeing not whither to go, but only feeling its own unhappiness and fear.

The resources of the calm man are superior to all incidents which may befall him. Nothing can alarm him, nothing can find him unprepared, nothing can shake his strong and steadfast mind. Wheresoever duty may call him, there will his strength manifest itself; there will his mind, free from the frictions of self, exhibit its silent and patient power. Whether he be engaged in things worldly or things spiritual, he will do his work with concentrated vigour and penetrating insight.

Calmness means that the mind is harmoniously adjusted, perfectly poised. All its extremes once so antagonistic and painful are reconciled, merged into one grand central principle with which the mind has identified itself. It means that the runaway passions are tamed and subjected, the intellect is purified, and the will is merged into the Cosmic Will. That is, it is no longer centred upon narrow personal ends, but is concerned with the good of all.

A man is not wholly victorious until he is perpetually calm. While passing things disturb him, his understanding is unripe, his heart is not altogether pure. A man cannot advance in the triumph of life while he flatters and deceives himself. He must awake, and be fully alive to the fact that his sins, sorrows, and troubles are of his own making, and belong to his own imperfect condition. He must understand that his miseries have their root in his own sins, and not in the sins of others. He must strive after calmness as the covetous man strives after riches; and he must not rest satisfied with any partial attainment. He will thus grow in grace and wisdom, in strength and peace, and calmness will descend upon his spirit as the refreshing dew descends upon the flowers.

Where the calm mind is, there is strength and rest, there is love and wisdom. There is one who has fought successfully innumerable battles against self, who, after long toil in secret against his own failings, has triumphed at last.

8

Insight and Nobility

In the pursuit and practice of virtue, there at last comes a time when a divine insight dawns upon the mind. It searches into the causes and principles of things, which, once attained, establishes its possessor firmly in virtue. It renders him invulnerable to the assaults of temptation, and invincible in his work for the world.

When the understanding is ripened by the culture of virtue, vicious inclinations disappear, and wrong-doing becomes impossible. When individual conduct is perceived as an unbroken series of causes and effects, the perceiving mind finally decides for virtue, and the lower selfish elements are just cast away forever.

Until a man perceives the just law which operates in human life, whatever virtue he may manifest at any given time, he is not firmly established in nobility of character, he is not fully armored with righteousness, and is not safely lodged in his final refuge. Not having acquired that perfect insight which knows good and evil and which perceives the effects of all deeds both good and bad, he breaks down when assailed by temptation at those points in his character which are not well fortified. Those which have, so far, dimmed his spiritual insight, and barred him from perfect vision. By thus breaking down, he discovers that within which has hindered him. And by setting to work to remove the hindrance, he ascends still higher in the scale of virtue, and approaches nearer to the perfect insight into the true order of life which makes a man divine.

Under certain circumstances a man, held in restraint by the influence of friends, by custom and environment, and not by his own inherent purity and strength, will appear to have, and may believe he possesses, a virtue of which he knows nothing in reality. And his lack of such virtue only appears when all outward restraints are withdrawn, and, under temptation, the concealed weakness and vice make themselves manifest.

On the other hand, the man of superior virtue will seem, in a familiar environment, to be much the same as his weaker fellows, and his virtue will not be apparent to those about him. But when he is suddenly brought in contact with great temptations or extraordinary events, his latent virtue appears in all its beauty and strength.

Insight destroys the dominion of evil and reveals the faultless operation of the Good Law. The man of perfect insight cannot sin, because he fully understands the nature of good and evil. And it is impossible for one who knows good and evil, in all their ramifications of cause and effect, to choose the evil and reject the good. Just as the sane man would not choose ashes in preference to food, so the spiritually awakened man would not choose evil in preference to good. The presence of sin is an indication of self-delusion and of ignorance; the spiritual vision is warped or undeveloped, and there is confusion of mind concerning the nature of good and evil.

In the early stages of virtue, a man arrays himself against the forces of evil which appear to him to be overpowering in their might, and almost, if not entirely, unconquerable. But with the advent of insight, a new light is thrown upon the nature of things, and evil appears as it actually is—a small, dark, powerless thing, a mere negation, and not a formidable force or combination of forces. The man of insight knows that the root of evil is ignorance—and not an intelligent power—and that all sin and suffering proceed therefrom. Thus, knowing evil to be merely a depravation of good, he cannot hate it, but manifests compassion for all sinning and suffering beings.

Indeed, he who has so far conquered the evil in his own heart, as to know the nature and source of evil, cannot possibly hate, dislike, or despise any being, no matter how far removed from virtue it may be. But, while fully perceiving the degradation of character, he understands the dark spiritual condition from which such degradation springs, and so he pities and helps where, without insight, he would hate and despise. Love ever attends upon insight, and pity waits on knowledge.

That insight which proceeds from self-purification and long acquaintance with virtue makes itself manifest in the form of ripeness of character. There is an unchanging strength and sweetness combined; a clearness of intellect, a virile strength of will and a gentleness of heart—a combination which denotes a cultured, mellowed, perfected being; one who has acquired sympathy, compassion, purity, and wisdom. Thus, while "Goodness gives insight," insight renders goodness permanent, fixes the mind in the love and practice of all that is pure and noble, and stamps upon man's brow the seal of divinity.

The man whose goodness is of the kind that does not alter with altered environment, or with the changing attitudes of those around him, has reached the Divine Goodness; he understands the Supreme Good. He is no longer concerned with evil as a thing that can harm, but he is concerned with good only. And so he ignores evil and recognizes only good. He perceives that men commit evil out of the mistaken idea of good, and, thus perceiving, no hatred against any can enter his peaceful heart.

The life of such a man is powerful, no matter how obscure it may be, for goodness is the most powerful thing in the world. The fact of his living and moving among men confers incalculable benefit upon the race, although during his lifetime this may not be perceived or understood. So powerful is goodness that the destiny of the world was, is, and will be in the hands of the good.

Those who are good are the guides and emancipators of humanity. In the present period of its development, they are taking the race rapidly along in its evolutionary journey; and this, not in any mystical or miraculous sense, but in a very practical and normal sense, by their exemplary lives, by the power of their deeds. The good men who help the world are not wonder-workers, though undeveloped minds have ever tried to make them such—but the workers of righteousness, servants of the Good Law.

The world never was, is not, and will not be, under the dominion of evil, for such a condition would mean non-existence, evil being merely the negation of good, as darkness is the negation of light. It is light, and not darkness which is the sustaining power. Evil is the weakest thing in the world, and cannot accomplish anything. The universe not only makes for good, the universe is good, and evil always falls short and fails.

Insight is seeing in the Light of Truth, that Light which is the revealer of all things. As the light of day reveals all objects in the world in their proper forms, so when the Light of Truth enters the mind it reveals all the things of life in their proper proportions. He who searches his own heart by the aid of Truth, searches all hearts. He who, by long searching, has perceived the Perfect Law which is operative in his mind, has revealed the Divine Law which is the stay and substance of the universe.

Insight disperses error and puts an end to superstition. Sin is the only error, Men attack each other's beliefs and remain in ignorance. When they get rid of their own sins they will become enlightened.

Superstition springs from sin. Looking through darkened eyes, men see evil things which are delusions of ignorance; conceiving in their hearts unlawful things, their imagination is troubled with monsters and terrors which have no existence in reality. Where there is pure insight there is no fear. Devils, demons, wrathful and jealous gods, vampires and evil spirits, and all the hideous host of the ideological monsters, have vanished from the universe along with the feverish nightmare which gave them birth. And before the rapt gaze of the purified one there spreads a universe of orderly beauty and inviolate law.

The man of insight lives in the beatific vision of the saints, not as a fleeting experience in a moment of exceptional purity, but as a constant, normal condition of mind. He has completed his long journey through self and sorrow, and is at peace. He has conquered, and is glad.

He sees all the sin, misery, and pain that are in the world more plainly and vividly than other men. But he now sees it as it is in its cause, inception, growth, and fruitage, not as it appeared to him when he was blindly involved in it, and his mind was distorted by impurities.

He watches the growth of beings, from the immature to the mature, through periods of change and pain, with tender compassion and solicitude, as the mother watches the growth of her child through the helpless period of its infancy.

He sees justice operating in all things. While men are waxing wrathful over the triumph of wrong, he knows that wrong has not triumphed, but is brought to naught. He sees the overruling Right which, though concealed from worldly eyes, remains forever unshaken. He sees the littleness, the puny weakness, the blind folly of evil as compared with the majesty, the invincible power, and the all-seeing wisdom of Good. And thus, knowing and seeing, his mind is finally fixed in that which is good. He is devoted to Truth, and his delight is in the doing of righteousness.

When insight is born in the mind, Reality stands revealed; not a metaphysical reality distinct from the universe; not a speculative reality other than the things of life, but the Reality of the universe itself, the Reality of "things-in-themselves." Insight is triumphant over change and decay, for it perceives the abiding in change, the eternal in the transient, the immortal in the things which pass away.

And herein is the meaning of that fixed nobility of character of the saints and sages, and superlatively, of the Great Teachers of the Race—that they perceive and abide in Reality. They know life in its completion; they understand and obey the Righteous Law. Having conquered self, they have conquered all delusions; have triumphed over sin, they have triumphed over sorrow; having purified themselves, they see the Perfect Cosmos.

He who chooses the right, the pure, the good, and clings to them through all misunderstandings, insults, and defeat, reaches, at last, the place of insight, and his eyes open upon the world of truth. Then his painful discipline is ended; the lower conditions no more affect him or cause him sorrow. Purity and joy abide with him, and the universe again rejoices in the triumph of good, and hails another conqueror.

9

Man the Master

By the mastery of self, a distinct form of consciousness is evolved which some would call divine. It is distinguished from that ordinary human consciousness, which craves personal advantages and gratifications on the one hand, and is involved in remorse and sorrow on the other. This divine consciousness concerns itself with humanity and the universe, with eternal verities, with righteousness, wisdom, and truth, and not with pleasures, protection, and preservation of the personality. Not that personal pleasure is destroyed, but that it is no longer craved and sought, it no longer takes a foremost place. It is purified, and it is received as the effect of right thought and action, and is no longer an end in itself.

In divine consciousness there is neither sin nor sorrow. Even the sense of sin has passed away, and the true order and purpose of life being revealed, no cause is found for lamentation. Jesus called this state of consciousness "The Kingdom of Heaven"; Buddha named it "Nirvana"; Lao-Tze's term for it was "Tao"; Emerson refers to it as "The Over-Soul"; and Dr. Bucke calls it "Cosmic Consciousness" in his valuable work bearing that title.

The ordinary human consciousness is self-consciousness. Self, the personality, is placed before everything else. There are ceaseless anxieties and fears concerning the self. Its possible loss is thought to be the most grievous calamity, and its eternal preservation the most important thing in the universe.

In divine consciousness all this has passed away. Self has disappeared. Therefore, there can be no more fears and anxieties concerning the self, and things are considered and known as they are, and not as they afford pleasure or cause pain to self, not as self wishes them to be for its own temporal or eternal happiness.

The self-conscious man is subject to desire; the divinely conscious man is master of desire. The former considers what is pleasant or unpleasant; the latter acts from the righteous law without reference to pleasure or pain.

The race is passing through self-consciousness to divine consciousness; through the slavery of self, with its sense of sin and shame, to the freedom of Truth, with its sense of purity and power. The Great Teachers and Saviours of the race have already attained. In former existences they have already passed through all forms of self-consciousness, and now, having subjugated self, have become divinely conscious.

They have reached the summit of evolution on this earth, and have no further need to be reborn in the self-conscious form. They are Masters of Life. Having conquered self, they have acquired the Supreme Knowledge. Some of them are worshiped as God because they manifest a wisdom and a consciousness which is quite distinct from the normal self-consciousness of humanity, and which is therefore regarded with, and surrounded by, incomprehensible mystery. Yet, in this divine consciousness there is no mystery, but, on the contrary, a transparent simplicity which becomes apparent when the confusions of self are dispersed.

The abiding gentleness, the sublime wisdom, the perfect calm of the Great Teachers—qualities which appear supernatural when viewed from the self-consciousness state—are seen to be simple and natural when the first glimmering of divine consciousness dawns in the mind. And such divine consciousness does not appear until a high degree of morality is attained by self-conscious man.

Man becomes divinely conscious, divinely wise, divinely gentle and strong in the measure that he subdues and dominates within, those passions by which humanity is subdued and dominated. The divine master is one who has attained mastery over self. The abiding nobility, beneficent characteristics, and unobtrusive virtue which mark off the spiritually enlightened man from others, are the fruits of self-conquest, the logical outcome of a long struggle to master and comprehend those mental forces which the self-conscious man blindly obeys without understanding.

Self-conscious man is a slave to self. Obeying self-centred inclinations, he is in submission to his passions, and to the sorrows and pains which allegiance to those passions inflict upon him. He is conscious of sin and sorrow, but sees no way out of these conditions. And so he invents theologies which he substitutes for effort, and which, while affording him fitful comfort through uncertain hope, leave him the easy victim of sin, and the willing prey of sorrow.

Divinely conscious man is the master of self. He obeys Truth and not self. He curbs and directs his inclinations and is conscious of a growing power over sin and sorrow. He sees that there is a way out of these conditions by the path of self-mastery. He needs no theologies to aid him, but exerts himself in right-doing, and is gladdened by a sense of victory and increasing purity and power. When his mastery is complete, he has no inclinations but those which accord with Truth. He has then become the conqueror of sin, and is no longer subject to sorrow.

Enlightened, wise, and evermore peaceful and happy is he who has subjected, overcome, and cast out the turbulent self that reigned within. The tempests of sorrow do not chill him. The cares and troubles which beset man pass him by, and no evil thing overtakes him. Secure in divine virtue, no enemy can overthrow him; no foe can do harm.

Kind and peaceful, no person, power, nor place can rob him of repose.

There is no enemy but self, no darkness but ignorance, no suffering but that which springs from the insubordinate elements of one's own nature.

No man is truly wise who is involved in likes and dislikes, wishes and regrets, desires and disappointments, sins and sorrow. All these conditions belong to the self-conscious state, and are indications of folly, weakness, and subjection.

He is truly wise who, in the midst of worldly duties, is always calm, always gentle, always patient. He accepts things as they are, and does not wish nor grieve, desire nor regret. These things belong to the divinely conscious state, the dominion of Truth, and are indications of enlightenment, strength, and mastery.

He who does not desire riches, fame, or pleasures; who enjoys what he has, yet does not lament when it is taken from him, he is indeed wise.

He who desires riches, fame, and pleasure; who is discontented with what he has, yet laments when it is taken from him, he is indeed foolish.

Man is fitted for conquest, but the conquest of territory will not avail; he must resort to the conquest of self. The conquest of territory renders man a temporal ruler, but the conquest of self makes him an eternal conqueror.

Man is destined for mastery; not the mastery of his fellow men by force, but the mastery of his own nature by self-control. The mastery of his fellow men by force is the crown of egotism, but the mastery of self by self-control is the crown of humility.

He is man the master who has shaken off the service of self for the service of Truth, who has established himself in the Eternal Verities. He is crowned, not only with perfect manhood, but with divine wisdom. He has overcome the disturbances of the mind and the shocks of life. He is superior to all circumstances. He is the calm spectator, but no longer the helpless tool, of events. No more a sinning, weeping, repenting mortal, he is pure, rejoicing, upright immortal. He perceives the course of things with a glad and peaceful heart; a divine conqueror, master of life and death.

10

Knowledge and Victory

Faith is the beginning of the Triumphant Life, but knowledge is its consummation. Faith reveals the way, but knowledge is the goal. Faith suffers many afflictions; knowledge has transcended affliction. Faith endures; knowledge loves. Faith walks in darkness, but believes; knowledge acts in light, and knows. Faith inspires to effort; knowledge crowns effort with success. "Faith is the substance of things hoped for"; knowledge is the substance of those things possessed. Faith is the helpful staff of the pilgrim; knowledge is the City of Refuge at the journey's end. Without faith there will be no knowledge, but when knowledge is acquired, the work of faith is finished.

The Life Triumphant is a life of knowledge; and by knowledge is meant, not booklearning, but life-learning; not superficial facts committed to memory, but the deep facts and truths of life, grasped and comprehended. Apart from this knowledge there is no victory for man, no rest for his weary feet, no refuge for His aching heart.

There is no salvation for the foolish except by becoming wise. There is no salvation for the sinful except by becoming pure. There is no liberation for man from the turmoil and troubles of life but through divine knowledge reached by the pathway of a pure and blameless life. Nowhere is there permanent peace except in an enlightened condition of mind; and a pure life and an enlightened mind are identical.

But there is salvation for the foolish because wisdom can be acquired. There is salvation for the sinful because purity can be embraced. There is liberation for all men from the troubles and turmoil of life because whosoever wills to do so—whether rich or poor, learned or unlearned—can enter the lowly way of blamelessness which leads to perfect knowledge. And because of this—that there is deliverance for the captives and victory for the defeated—there is rejoicing in the High Places, and the universe is glad.

The man of knowledge, being victorious over himself, is victorious over sin, over evil, over all the disharmonies of life. Out of the old mind marred by sin and sorrow, he has framed a new mind glorified by purity and peace. He has died out of the old world of evil, and is reborn in a new world where love and faultless law prevail, where evil is not, and he has become deathless in immortal Good.

Anxiety and fear, grief and lamentation, disappointment and regret, wretchedness and remorse—these things have no part in the world of the wise. They are the shadowy inhabitants of the world of self, and cannot five, nay, they are seen to have no substantiality—in the light of wisdom. The dark things of life are the dark conditions of a mind not yet illuminated by the light of wisdom. They follow self as the shadow of substance. Where selfish desires go, there they follow; where sin is, there they are. There is no rest in self; there is no light in self. And where the flames of turbulent passions and fires of consuming desires are rife, the cool airs of wisdom and peace are not felt.

Safety and assurance, happiness and repose, satisfaction and contentment, joy and peace—these are the abiding possessions of the wise, earned by right of self-conquest, the results of righteousness, the wages of a blameless life.

The substance of a right life is enlightenment (knowledge), and the spirit of knowledge is peace. To be victorious over self in all the issues of life is to know life as it is in reality, and not as it appears in the nightmare of self. It is to be in peace in all passages, and not to be stricken with trouble and grief in the common happenings of life.

As the ripe scholar is no more troubled by incorrect work and lessons imperfectly done, and the painful reproof and punishment formerly inflicted by his teachers are left behind forever, so the perfected scholar in virtue, the wise man and woman, the enlightened doer of righteousness, is no more troubled with wrongdoing and folly (which are merely the imperfectly accomplished lessons of life), and the scourging of sorrow and remorse have passed away forever.

The skilled scholar has no more doubt or fear concerning his ability. He has overcome and dispersed the ignorance of his intellect. He has attained to learning, and he knows that he has attained. And he so knows because, having undergone innumerable tests in the forms of lessons and examinations, he has at last proved his skill by passing successfully through the severest tests of scholarship. And now he no longer fears, but rejoices when severe tests are applied to prove his ability. He is capable, confident, and glad.

Even so the skilled doer of righteousness is no more troubled with doubt and fear concerning his destiny. He has overcome and dispersed the ignorance of his heart. He has attained to wisdom, and he knows that he has attained. And he so knows because where he formerly failed and fell when tested by the wrong conduct of others, he now maintains his patience and calmness under the severest tests of accusation and reproof.

Herein is the glory and victory of divine knowledge, that understanding the nature of deeds, both good and bad, the enlightened doer of good deeds no longer suffers through the bad deeds of others. Their actions towards him can never cause him pain and sorrow, nor rob him of his peace. Having taken refuge in good, evil can no more reach nor harm him. He returns good for evil, and overcomes the weakness of evil by the power of good.

The man who is involved in bad deeds imagines that the bad deeds of others are powerful to do him injury and are filled with grievous harm against him. He is stung with pain and overwhelmed with sorrow, not for his own bad deeds (for these he does not see) but for the wrong deeds of others. Involved in ignorance, he has no spiritual strength, no refuge, and no abiding peace.

The man victorious over self is the true seer. He is not the seer of spirits or supernatural phenomena, for such seeing is narrow and illusory. He is the seer of life as it is, both in its particular aspects and in its divine principles; the seer of the spiritual universe of cosmic law, cosmic love, and cosmic liberty.

The man of knowledge and victory, who has shaken off the painful dreams of self, has awakened with a new vision which beholds a new and glorified universe, He is the seer of the Eternal, and is blessed with perfect love and endless peace. He is lifted far above all sordid desires, narrow aims, and selfish love and hate; and being so lifted up he perceives the lawful course of things, and does not grieve when overtaken by the inevitable. He is above the world of sorrow, not because he has become cold and cruel, but because he abides in a love where no thought of self can enter, and where the well-being of others is all-in-all. He is sorrowless because he is selfless. He is serene because he knows that whatever he receives, it is good, and whatever is taken from him, that also is good. He has transmuted sorrow into love, and is filled with infinite tenderness and abounding compassion. His power is not violent, ambitious, worldly, but pure, peaceful, heavenly, and he is possessed of a hidden strength which knows how to stand and when to bend for the good of others and the world.

He is a Teacher, though he speaks but little. He is a Master, yet he has no desire to rule others. He is a Conqueror, but makes no attempt to subdue his fellow men. He has become a conscious instrument for the outworking of cosmic law, and is an intelligent, enlightened power directing the evolution of the Race.

At this, the beginning of a new epoch, let the Good News again go forth throughout the world that there is purity for the sinful, comfort for the afflicted, healing for the broken-hearted, and triumph for the defeated. In your heart, O man! O woman! stained as it is with sin, and torn with conflicting desires, there is a place of power, a citadel of strength. You are the dwelling-place of the Supreme Good, and the Scepter of Victory awaits you: deep in your consciousness is the High Seat of Empire. Arise, O stricken one! Ascend your rightly throne!